ISSUE 3

NOVEMBER 2017

Marisa Wohlschlaeger

Marisa Wohlschlaeger

LOUD & QUEER

QUEER VOICES OF NOW

QUEER STRIFE, QUEER LIFE

Marisa Wohlschlaeger

QUEER STRIFE, QUEER LIFE

Living as an LGTBQIA+ person is a unique experience with positive and negative hues.

Many of us have known the strife of not being accepted by society, hiding who we are, and even coming to dislike the queer side of ourselves. At different levels, in different nations, under different laws, we all share this hardship.

But queer life is so much more than that. Being LGBTQIA+ brings us joys and experiences that we would never trade. The kinship we feel when we meet someone else in the community is electric. The comfort we feel when the community supports us gives us new strength. The rush of a new connection renews the joy of life.

This issue explores QUEER STRIFE, QUEER LIFE, with pictures , moments, and memories from LGBTQIA+ voices. Because queer life encompasses beauty and pain, the zine includes some content that isn't suitable for everyone. Please note the content warnings in the table of contents and at the top of each page.

Thank you for being a part of the LOUD & QUEER COMMUNITY. Your interest and support is what allows us to create this zine and share queer voices of now.

 @LOUDANDQUEERZINE

 @LOUDANDQUEERZINE

 @LOUDANDQUEERZ

LOUDANDQUEERZINE@GMAIL.COM

CONTENTS

Content Warning Legend

[1] Violence   [2] Suicide   [3] Explicit Language

[4] Nudity   [5] Drugs

Space

By Rhian Williams

She is counterpoint to my supernova,
I am a brilliant point of light
burnt out before my time
and she is the only thing
I am holding onto
as I blaze through existence.
She is my solar system.
briefly I outshine her
mere moments pass
but she is my gravity and harmony
and I deny her nothing.
She leads and I follow,
through every hindrance
as through every asteroid field
were made of pebbles
to be pushed aside as we sail on
and I suffer less as she carries me forward
through stardust and nebulas
home and back again, a galaxy of wonder
under our countenance
two little gems in the middle of
this superficial extent.

Pluck

By Rhian Williams

I haven't quite decided
what they tell me is true
pluck away one by one
and leave me hanging by my bones
my soul scoured clean and raw
by every touch.
Probably should've listened
but here I am all the same
We are here all the same
put off for too long
the burn is equalled
in desperation
mine and yours
and the push is exquisite but
I'm too broken.
Probably should've done this
a long time ago.
All this time wasted
and now I still can't quite decide
if I should pull away
or brush it aside
but piece by piece I'm coming apart.
Put me back together or leave,
we can't do both
and it doesn't matter anyway.

Remains

By Rhian Williams

It's all embers now,
all ash and breath
and nothing else left.
I mourn for memories
I haven't even lost
as I fall to sleep
in the growing grass
little shoots making themselves known
in the dirt and ruin
at our feet,
soon covered over and washed away
waves roll in and out
between full moons,
broken sunshine
cloudy skies and aching hearts.
Watch until it's all gone
not a trace,
not even remains.

Note from the author:

A weird poet, geek and blogger from the edge of nowhere Wales. Bi, non-binary and writing about everything on queerlittlefamily.co.uk and www.scruffy-duck.net

CW: None

Queer Queries: Should LGBT+ come under one title?

By Molly

Should LGBT come under all one bracket of gender and sexuality? Should the two, which are so easily confused, be forever put in to one collective title?

As a child, I was brought up believing that sex and gender were essentially the same thing. It was not until my teenage years i learnt that there was a distinct difference between sexual orientation and gender. It was at that point that I learnt about the LGBT+ community. It was only then, age 13, that I learnt about any kind of other sexual orientation.

I believe that by putting both gender and sexuality under one label it can be confusing to distinguish between the two, meaning that from a young age children believe the two are synonymous. If we were to put them under two separate labels would it make it easier to teach children and educate the next generation on this vital difference? Or is the problem easily solved, not by labels, but simply by educating our youngsters in more depth from a younger age?

Note from the author:

My name is Molly and I am a pansexual female. I love to write about and support the LGBTQ+ community, as well as taking part in different activities locally.

Husband

By Adam Martinez

Dating, we all think it's going to be easy. When growing up we are told we would meet "the one" that would sweep us off our feet. Once you've met that person you would just know and everything would work out. TV and movies lead us to believe that no matter the obstacle we all would get that happy ending. As if all you really need is love? No one ever stops to consider who it may be you fall for. Every person has a different story, some stories that may remain a secret. In some cases you meet that person when you are young so when it comes to that story you're the main character. Then most of us meet someone when we are much older this giving us more of a past.

But what does a person's story have to do with you?

When it came to dating for me it was always a different type of story. So believe me when I say nothing comes easy. I always seemed to attract the bi-curious or down-low men, in other terms. When it comes to these types of men we often wonder what it is that makes them hide. Is it what their family might say? Or could it just be the fear of how their friends or others might treat them? It takes a strong man to admit his sexuality and live life the way he wants. Yet that doesn't seem to hold any of them back from fulfilling that gay fantasy.

I knew this married couple, let's just call them Husband and Wife. We had been friends for many years. It was a type of friendship that knew no boundaries. Wife and I had always been very close and as the years went on Husband and I developed a certain connection. For the most part I never questioned it nor did I seek anything more, until one night at a club Husband made a pass at me. Yes, he made the first move and let me say I was more than shocked.

That night Husband and I took our friendship to a new level, we had sex. Now I wouldn't say he cheated on Wife since she was there. Let me say it was a threesome neither of us expected. For the first few weeks things seemed weird with them. We didn't hang out as often, plus we didn't speak like we usually would. Finally Husband reached out to me and we all hung out. I learned that nothing had changed between us. In fact we seemed to have grown closer.

One day Wife told me of an article she had read about a married couple that had taken in a boyfriend. In that instance he dated them both, since both men were bisexual. For Wife she was looking for something different. She wanted a best friend she could hang out with while he dated her Husband. Apparently she did love her Husband, but loved watching two guys more. Makes you think right?

So what did I do?

I decided to try this out and see where it could lead. Husband was a good guy, one that always seemed to make me happy. From what I knew he felt the same way about way me. So begins the time I dated a bi-curious man, well also a married man. Of course this was meant to be our little secret. Most people wouldn't understand that there was real love between he and I.

When it comes to love and marriage religion leads us to believe it must be between a man and a woman. Most people would freak out, not take the time to understand that love knows no sex, nor does it judge. So why are we taught that? Why as children must we be told what is right or wrong when it comes to who you love? I was never one to stay within the mold society put me in.

Husband and I began a relationship. Most nights it would be me just hanging out with them at their house. A few times he and I would go out you know a bar here, a drive there. Every night would end with just he and I. Although no one knew of what we had. He wanted to keep us a secret. He came from a close family with catholic values. For months I felt as though I was on top of the world. I had found a man that loved me and now had a friend that understood me. The three of us felt we had overcome what the world expected from us. We had a relationship and two people to count on.

I know some gay men would kill for this to be their story, while some women longed to have their gay best friend at their side. Only things aren't always so happy and worth the hiding. So when I say hiding that meant I was never really a part of that couple. For Wife, I was the one having sex with Husband keeping her from having to, plus we did all the friend things together. Husband had that person he could rely on and not to mention get sex whenever he wanted.

To me it felt I had been more, but in a threesome it may not always be what you expect.

When it came to dating Husband the relationship had its limitations. It began to seem as if I were just a play thing for them, someone to live out a need. When you become that guest star in a relationship that's what you are, a guest. Although Husband was curious about being with me and he had been willing to date me, at his level. There was still the fact that I held no true place at their side.

Dating someone you feel they would be the one person you knew would always be there, but when dating a bi-curious man you would find you are something different. Yes you were one of the best friends and yes you knew more about them than anyone else. Only did that really matter? For me I had nothing but love for him and he would be the one I'd be faithful to. Only at times you wondered where you really fit into the equation. Sometimes if you date a bi-curious man you may not consistently be at his side, as his girlfriend would be, you may just be that "friend" they hung out with. That was another thing you may not get is the boyfriend title.

As the months went on the going out with Husband turned into us all just hanging out at their house. The nights of passion turned into a quickie in the garage or a fast blow job in the backyard. The fantasy of dating a bi-curious married man was now being his sexual release. Not to mention the fact Wife preferred to watch us as she masturbated. Ironically now that I was in the picture she no longer wanted to have sex with Husband. It wasn't what I wanted more what kept them both comfortable and satis-fied, which made sense the marriage suffered once the boyfriend was gone.

When it came to this certain relationship, I dated a bi-curious married man for a few months. Now I'm not saying that your story would end this way, but mine did. Every person has a story and every story has a differ-ent outcome. For Husband, he saw me as just someone that came to help fulfill his curiosity of being with a man, plus to give him consistent sexual relief.

In the next story we will see what it's like when emotions are more in-volved. Will you be able to call this love? Or would dating a bi-curious man always just be a fantasy???

X

By Adam Martinez

Relationships, what really defies one? When you meet someone you both decide to form a union between the two of you. It is a commitment that no one else will come between, but when two friends of the same sex create this what does it really mean? While growing up we are brain washed to believe it will have to be between a man and a woman, but what if those men secretly like men? You know the down low or bi-curious men. Can they truly have a relationship with another man? Maybe seeing it as a bromance makes it a little easier for them to go through with it. However you chose to look at it, it's still dating.

I had this friend I'll just call X. X was someone I counted on for a lot, as did he did with me. In the beginning the motions were ones of just a friendship, yet as time went on we learned it could be more. If he needed someone to vent to, I was there. If I needed a shoulder to cry on he would hold me. For the first few years of our friendship we build this bond that most men didn't have with another man, with me being gay and he straight that was a given.

The first night I realized things with X were different was when he had been badly blown off by a girl. That night we drank until he couldn't drink anymore then we crashed. I held him all night as he held onto me. X was a good guy, an attractive one too, but for some reason he picked the wrong girls. Makes you think right? Every girl he dated seemed to want nothing more than just sex from him. Ironically for a man his heart was always on his shoulder, or maybe he was really looking for something a woman couldn't give him?

Let's fast forward to three months later. X was trying to be a man all about the girls. You know those types. Strip clubs, random hook ups, and getting girls to cheat on their man with you. I felt as though he was now taking a new path to find a girl, only this night that didn't work. We ended up going back to his place where the night lead to hours of amazing, mind blowing sex. The kind of sex you've only heard about. So X never said he liked men nor did he ever say his sexuality, but I knew, he was bi-curious. The sex between us was way more than just a random thing, it felt as though it was a buildup of a strong connection between us that no one would admit.

Although the sex didn't happen as often as I had wanted, X made sure to treat me better than most men had before. He would take me out for drinks, dinner, sometimes even the movies. The nights we spent in he made sure to listen and still be that man I needed to count on, as I did for him. Our friendship seemed to advance to a new level, sadly that didn't last long.

Like most bi-curious men X would go back to women. Once that happened I was out of the picture and sometimes for a while. Only when the girl was gone X would come crawling back to me, the one person that would always be there. I never minded being that person for X it made me feel more fulfilled. The friendship we had was one that was much needed in life and one you would do anything for. We all have those friends that we call ride or die and X was the one man I learned I could truly count on, well at most times.

X never wanted to admit what we had was something real nor could he ever admit to having actual feelings for another man. One time when he was drunk he confessed his love for me and how he felt I was the one. He went on to explain that he never looked at a man the way he saw me. The truth was somehow he had fallen for me and I knew he was scared. Since I had first met X he always had the women, there was never a girl he couldn't get. When out, I'd see girls throw themselves at him along with his phone always going off. Some girl begging him to take her back or one needing him to satisfy her. We believe women view sex differently than men while being X's friend I learned some use men more. Sadly for X he was the type of guy that you had to have at least once, okay maybe twice.

The thing was I never treated X as some dick that could make me scream. He was always more to me and that I knew he felt. When we would be together he made sure I was always his main one, I was always the one he went to. Only for some reason once a girl showed any kind of interest he threw me out like the trash. The part that killed me the most was he even had the nerve to disappear and ignore me. As if I would expose him or ruin his current fling, but that always ended and he found his way back to me.

When that happened the dating and the nights of amazing sex would continue. He always made sure to spoil me and make me feel as if I was the one person he wanted to spend his life with. I was always the first person he called in the morning and the last one he would text before bed. It was funny that a man who considered himself straight treated me better than a man that was openly gay. X really did know how to make his other half someone that was more than just special, I was his everything. We never called each other boyfriends, just best friends.

It was funny though when we were together he made it very clear I couldn't see or have sex with anyone else. In fact he made sure I got everything I needed from a man. We took care of each other sexually, mentally, and honestly financially. We never wanted or needed a thing when together. Everyday we did all we could to keep each other happy. It was better than any relationship either of us had been in, at the time. Even though he could never admit he was bi-curious, or that we were dating, X really was a good boyfriend.

Only when it came to women he still couldn't say no. I felt X wanted us to work out only on his terms. For him he wanted to be able to go off and be with a woman when he needed. Then to have me there waiting for him when he wanted me back. For four years this went on. I dated X and no matter what he thought, he had a boyfriend. Bi-curious men sometime have a different idea of what it is to date or be with another man. Maybe I didn't know what it was to date a bi-curious man, yet.

X and I finally ended it all when he met a girl and they got married. That was it. For at least ten months we no longer spoke until one day he text me. We talked debating if we should try and be friends or work on us. Of course this lead to us hanging out and then he would be nothing but apologetic. X made sure I understood the why behind his hiding and that he would make me happy again. He would build up new promises and make plans for us. This time I knew to stay away but when he told me he loved me and needed me, I had to go back. If I had listened more closely I would have heard that drunk in his voice. X only admitted any feelings to me when he was drunk.

So we would meet up for drinks and as the drinking got heavier X would begin to talk about how much he needed me. Then once we got into his truck he started to cry and tell me that he doesn't know why he keeps pushing me away. Crying that I am the only person that has ever truly been there for him. We'd hung and he'd hold me begging me to forgive him and how he never wants me to leave again. Then we would go back to his place and we would have some of the best sex, I swear his neighbors had to have heard us a few times.

Every time we had sex I felt as though we grew closer together and what we had became stronger. The feeling I'd get when he touched me or I felt him deep inside showed me we were more then just friends. But there's only so much that moment of passion can give you until it's over. The moment we would finish X did seem a little distant only it was always the next day he started to wonder about us. This time he called me the next day trying to make an excuse as to why he told me all he did. He would always make sure to end the conversation with telling me I was his best friend, yeah I was more than that.

After a few days had passed we would be back to normal. He usually only acted a little nervous after anal sex, as if that was going too far. Yet he wouldn't feel bad to ask for oral sex every time I saw him. That was like most guys though for them to get head was a must, not that I am complaining. X just didn't seem to understand what was truly between us. Part of me felt he wanted a boyfriend yet was too afraid to give into his feeling for me. It seemed every time we got one step closer to actually being a couple he'd find a girl. Then he was gone and that's exactly what happened again.

X met a girl and he seemed to believe this was the "one". We spent weeks talking and arguing about the situation. I couldn't help but feel used, which I had no idea why he felt the same way. We both realized there was no reason to talk about this. Whatever X and I had was truly over.

We did have a different relationship honestly one we could never explain. Our story may never have a happy ending, but it ended. We both just stopped talking to each other and went on with our new lives.

Bi-curious men sometimes come with a lot of baggage. Very few know how to put it in the back of their minds while others continue to follow their paths. Each man sees a relationship with another man differently and soon we may not be able to tell what we really are. Then there are the men that truly are just curious maybe not ready for the physical side of the relationship. When it comes to dating, every guy is different. I wonder how far they would let their curiosity take them???

Relationships, what really defies one? When you meet someone you both decide to form a union between the two of you. It is a commitment that no one else will come between, but when two friends of the same sex create this what does it really mean? While growing up we are brain washed to believe it will have to be between a man and a woman, but what if those men secretly like men? You know the down low or bi-curious men. Can they truly have a relationship with another man? Maybe seeing it as a bromance makes it a little easier for them to go through with it. However you chose to look at it, it's still dating.

I had this friend I'll just call X. X was someone I counted on for a lot, as did he did with me. In the beginning the motions were ones of just a friendship, yet as time went on we learned it could be more. If he needed someone to vent to, I was there. If I needed a shoulder to cry on he would hold me. For the first few years of our friendship we build this bond that most men didn't have with another man, with me being gay and he straight that was a given.

The first night I realized things with X were different was when he had been badly blown off by a girl. That night we drank until he couldn't drink anymore then we crashed. I held him all night as he held onto me. X was a good guy, an attractive one too, but for some reason he picked the wrong girls. Makes you think right? Every girl he dated seemed to want nothing more than just sex from him. Ironically for a man his heart was always on his shoulder, or maybe he was really looking for something a woman couldn't give him?

Let's fast forward to three months later. X was trying to be a man all about the girls. You know those types. Strip clubs, random hook ups, and getting girls to cheat on their man with you. I felt as though he was now taking a new path to find a girl, only this night that didn't work. We ended up going back to his place where the night lead to hours of amazing, mind blowing sex. The kind of sex you've only heard about. So X never said he liked men nor did he ever say his sexuality, but I knew, he was bi-curious. The sex between us was way more than just a random thing, it felt as though it was a buildup of a strong connection between us that no one would admit.

Although the sex didn't happen as often as I had wanted, X made sure to treat me better than most men had before. He would take me out for drinks, dinner, sometimes even the movies. The nights we spent in he made sure to listen and still be that man I needed to count on, as I did for him. Our friendship seemed to advance to a new level, sadly that didn't last long.

Like most bi-curious men X would go back to women. Once that happened I was out of the picture and sometimes for a while. Only when the girl was gone X would come crawling back to me, the one person that would always be there. I never minded being that person for X it made me feel more fulfilled. The friendship we had was one that was much needed in life and one you would do anything for. We all have those friends that we call ride or die and X was the one man I learned I could truly count on, well at most times.

X never wanted to admit what we had was something real nor could he ever admit to having actual feelings for another man. One time when he was drunk he confessed his love for me and how he felt I was the one. He went on to explain that he never looked at a man the way he saw me. The truth was somehow he had fallen for me and I knew he was scared. Since I had first met X he always had the women, there was never a girl he couldn't get. When out, I'd see girls throw themselves at him along with his phone always going off. Some girl begging him to take her back or one needing him to satisfy her. We believe women view sex differently than men while being X's friend I learned some use men more. Sadly for X he was the type of guy that you had to have at least once, okay maybe twice.

The thing was I never treated X as some dick that could make me scream. He was always more to me and that I knew he felt. When we would be together he made sure I was always his main one, I was always the one he went to. Only for some reason once a girl showed any kind of interest he threw me out like the trash. The part that killed me the most was he even had the nerve to disappear and ignore me. As if I would expose him or ruin his current fling, but that always ended and he found his way back to me.

When that happened the dating and the nights of amazing sex would continue. He always made sure to spoil me and make me feel as if I was the one person he wanted to spend his life with. I was always the first person he called in the morning and the last one he would text before bed. It was funny that a man who considered himself straight treated me better than a man that was openly gay. X really did know how to make his other half someone that was more than just special, I was his everything. We never called each other boyfriends, just best friends.

It was funny though when we were together he made it very clear I couldn't see or have sex with anyone else. In fact he made sure I got everything I needed from a man. We took care of each other sexually, mentally, and honestly financially. We never wanted or needed a thing when together. Everyday we did all we could to keep each other happy. It was better than any relationship either of us had been in, at the time. Even though he could never admit he was bi-curious, or that we were dating, X really was a good boyfriend.

Only when it came to women he still couldn't say no. I felt X wanted us to work out only on his terms. For him he wanted to be able to go off and be with a woman when he needed. Then to have me there waiting for him when he wanted me back. For four years this went on. I dated X and no matter what he thought, he had a boyfriend. Bi-curious men sometime have a different idea of what it is to date or be with another man. Maybe I didn't know what it was to date a bi-curious man, yet.

X and I finally ended it all when he met a girl and they got married. That was it. For at least ten months we no longer spoke until one day he text me. We talked debating if we should try and be friends or work on us. Of course this lead to us hanging out and then he would be nothing but apologetic. X made sure I understood the why behind his hiding and that he would make me happy again. He would build up new promises and make plans for us. This time I knew to stay away but when he told me he loved me and needed me, I had to go back. If I had listened more closely I would have heard that drunk in his voice. X only admitted any feelings to me when he was drunk.

So we would meet up for drinks and as the drinking got heavier X would begin to talk about how much he needed me. Then once we got into his truck he started to cry and tell me that he doesn't know why he keeps pushing me away. Crying that I am the only person that has ever truly been there for him. We'd hung and he'd hold me begging me to forgive him and how he never wants me to leave again. Then we would go back to his place and we would have some of the best sex, I swear his neighbors had to have heard us a few times.

Every time we had sex I felt as though we grew closer together and what we had became stronger. The feeling I'd get when he touched me or I felt him deep inside showed me we were more then just friends. But there's only so much that moment of passion can give you until it's over. The moment we would finish X did seem a little distant only it was always the next day he started to wonder about us. This time he called me the next day trying to make an excuse as to why he told me all he did. He would always make sure to end the conversation with telling me I was his best friend, yeah I was more than that.

After a few days had passed we would be back to normal. He usually only acted a little nervous after anal sex, as if that was going too far. Yet he wouldn't feel bad to ask for oral sex every time I saw him. That was like most guys though for them to get head was a must, not that I am complaining. X just didn't seem to understand what was truly between us. Part of me felt he wanted a boyfriend yet was too afraid to give into his feeling for me. It seemed every time we got one step closer to actually being a couple he'd find a girl. Then he was gone and that's exactly what happened again.

X met a girl and he seemed to believe this was the "one". We spent weeks talking and arguing about the situation. I couldn't help but feel used, which I had no idea why he felt the same way. We both realized there was no reason to talk about this. Whatever X and I had was truly over.

We did have a different relationship honestly one we could never explain. Our story may never have a happy ending, but it ended. We both just stopped talking to each other and went on with our new lives.

Bi-curious men sometimes come with a lot of baggage. Very few know how to put it in the back of their minds while others continue to follow their paths. Each man sees a relationship with another man differently and soon we may not be able to tell what we really are. Then there are the men that truly are just curious maybe not ready for the physical side of the relationship. When it comes to dating, every guy is different. I wonder how far they would let their curiosity take them???

Note from the author:

I'm Adam Martinez a writer in M/M erotica genre along with being a blogger for Only Lads where I write a blog about dating bi-curious men.
Since publishing my first book last year I am now working on completing the second of me series called the The DL Diaries the next book is titled DL in the City.

Margins and Murmurations

By Otter Lieffe

Audio Version—https://soundcloud.com/otterlieffe/margins-and-murmurations-chapter-1

The old woman's body felt alive from the run. Her strong legs burned as they carried her along the uneven riverbank. At seventy-four years old, she knew she should be slowing down, should be curled up in front of the fire, but today as she left her home on the river, climbed over an ancient stile and pushed her way through a thick field of bracken, Ash felt younger than ever.

The sun was close to setting but the air was still as hot as midday. After a relentless summer, the land was bone dry—she couldn't even remember the taste of rain.

Leaning against a fence to catch her breath, she offered some water from her bottle to the land and took a sip herself. Despite the drought, there was an explosion of plant growth all around her: a thick green mat of bracken and nettles filled the valley and young birch trees pushed up towards the light, their delicate branches drooping with the lavender blooms of morning glories.

"It's so beautiful here," Ash said to no-one in particular.

A passing crow flying out from the distant forest answered her from above.

Hard to imagine that all of this was corn. Nothing but toxic mono-culture as far as I could walk.

She took a deep breath of warm air, thick with pollen. The land itself seemed to buzz with the hum of bees and crickets. Life is coming back though. Despite everything they did to us.

Ash unzipped her backpack and crouched down to collect some nettle tips for dinner, smiling a little as they stung her. At her age, she figured she'd be riddled with arthritis by now if it wasn't for her daily cup of nettle tea and her regular brush against their stinging leaves. Soon her dark, wrinkled fingers prickled all over with the familiar burn of histamine. When she had collected enough, Ash put her hands together intending to thank the nettles for their sacrifice, but as she did so, a bang rang out from the forest.

She jumped to her feet and yelped in surprise, her heart pounding in her chest.

Gunshots. And they're getting closer every day. But Ash knew there was nothing she could do about it. I've swallowed enough tear gas for this lifetime.

She scratched the stubble on her chin thoughtfully, looked up and stretched her hand out in front of her. Only four finger tips separated the setting sun and the forest ahead of her. About an hour or so until dark. I should get moving.

She slipped her pack on again and, pushing through the abundant plant life, she continued her journey to the forest. It was normally an hour's journey from Ash's little river boat to Pinar's place, the beautiful cabin they had built together at the edge of the woods. In this heat, it would take her almost two and she'd be lucky to get there before nightfall.

Having no way to contact each other, their visits were always unplanned, always unexpected, and yet somehow Ash and Pinar had never missed each other in the five years since they came to this land. Ash knew that when she arrived, the kettle would already be boiling or a pot of soup would have just been taken off the fire in anticipation. It was as if somehow, when one of them left their home, the forest and the river themselves passed on the message and beckoned the other to stay in theirs, to leave the firewood collecting to later, to just sit and wait.

Ash disappeared into the high undergrowth, walking along a narrow path of stomped-down plants they both maintained just by hiking back and forth every few days. Her back was wet with sweat and brambles scratched her arms, but she loved this walk and hummed quietly to herself.

It was almost completely dark when the path suddenly opened out and beyond her in the forest she could hear a kettle whistling.

Not a minute too soon.

As she turned the corner, she saw Pinar, sitting outside her home surrounded by candles, her green eyes glistening in the light.

As gorgeous as ever, Ash noticed.

Pinar was only fifteen years her junior, but despite all that they had been through together, her friend seemed to radiate with youth. She wore an elegant blue dress that night and her long hair cascaded over dark, bare shoulders. She stood and smiled as Ash arrived.

"I had a feeling you might turn up today."

Pinar waved at a candlelit wooden table and chairs laid out under an old oak.

"I'll just get the kettle. Make yourself at home."

She disappeared inside the little cabin and Ash could hear her busying around in the kitchen. Within a minute, she returned with a tray full of homemade snacks, a steaming teapot and a pitcher of water.

"Here we go, I made the blackberry cookies you like." Pinar bent to put the tray down on the table, stood up and turned to give her friend a hug.

But Ash was gone.

Her body stood just where Pinar had left her moments ago, but the brown-green eyes that stared back at her were completely vacant.

"Ash?" she asked, but there was no response. Her friend's breath was shallow, her olive skin, cold and clammy to the touch. She was there, but she wasn't.

"Where are you now, darling?" asked Pinar, picking up a blanket and calmly putting it over her friend's shoulders. She wasn't worried. She was used to this.

Ash was somewhere else—in another place and another time. More a traumatic flashback than a daydream and still much more than that, Pinar knew she was visiting, or revisiting her own life.

"Be safe and come back to me soon," she said and sat down to pour tea.

—-

Ash saw herself running.

She stood in the middle of a road, soaked by a thick blanket of fog that hugged the asphalt. It was a cold, wet night and in the distance, she saw herself, younger in a long black dress, hand in hand with Pinar, running towards the open gates of the City.

Fuck, not again.

It was five years earlier and Ash remembered every painful detail.

A line of uniformed State troopers ran close behind, shouting and firing their guns into the air as they charged forward. The streets were lined with angry crowds who yelled and threw bottles and bags of rubbish at the two women as they passed.

"Get out of our city, perverts!" they shouted and even from that distance, Ash could see herself crying as she stumbled on a crack in the pavement. Pinar pulled her up and they ran on, towards the gate. My god. How we ran.

Standing unseen in the middle of the road, Ash knew there was nothing she could do here. She could barely breathe and her body was racked with shivers, from the cold or fear, she couldn't tell which. She wished desperately, with every taut muscle in her body, to escape this cycle, to stop reliving this trauma. But she had no control. She never did.

She saw that the troops had stopped running and her younger self and Pinar were nowhere to be seen. They had escaped the City, had fled into the darkness of the forest. The massive gates began to swing closed and the troops, and the people, whooped and yelled in victory.

Ash was struck with nausea and she could feel herself spinning. The shouts of men began to fade as the world itself, colours and smells and sounds, began to fade away from her.

It's always like this, she told herself. I'm going back.

Note from the author:

Written by a trans woman and sex worker, Margins and Murmurations puts transgender, sex work and femininity at the centre of its twisting, multi-layered narrative. In this sensitive exploration of exclusion, intimacy and control, Otter Lieffe calls us to renew our struggles against oppression and to proudly reclaim the margins that so many of us call home. Otter is a working class, femme, trans activist currently living in Brussels where she runs a trans and queer focused holistic clinic called Safer Healing. Margins and Murmurations is her first novel. Learn more—https://otterlieffe.com/

Small Town Boy

By Patric Stillman

I Am

By Patric Stillman

Who Wants to Live Forever

By Patric Stillman

Note from the author:

Regardless of the passage of time, the personal impact of the AIDS epidemic continues to fuel my creative drive. As a gay man who came of age during the early 80s, my entire world was put askew. I felt the lost without the elders of the community. So many creative mentors of my generation were robbed of their voices. It was a difficult entry into adulthood as I found myself surrounded by a community fearful of opening themselves up to new relationships as they watched their friends and loved ones die. Meanwhile, the rest of the country seemed especially cruel and uncaring as I watched the epidemic take my own friends.

Now, as a mature man, the sadness and anger of the past has forged into a desire to step up as a creative mentor of a sort. I have a burning need to create art that presents my truth honestly and openly in hopes that it will offer a sense of continuity and connectedness for others to accept themselves so that they can explore all that they can be. After all, in spite of progress for the LGBTQIA community, coming to terms with one's own identity remains a personal struggle.

Pride and Protest

By Patric Stillman

Note from the author cont'd:

These works are from my exhibition PERSON PLACE OR THING, which places a spotlight on gay male identity using the visual iconography of film noir. Extraordinarily stylized, noir is the perfect vehicle to express the ideas within my work. The heavily shadowed black and white worlds represent a heightened form of reality. It brings the psychological themes of obsession, sexuality, disillusionment and alienation. Tripped by fate, hardboiled anti-heroes are placed into the night, which translates as the perfect allegory for homosexuality while also reversing the noir genre's poor representation of the community as victims and undesirables.

CW: Nudity

Atria

By Patrick Moran

Carnival of Mirrors

By Patrick Moran

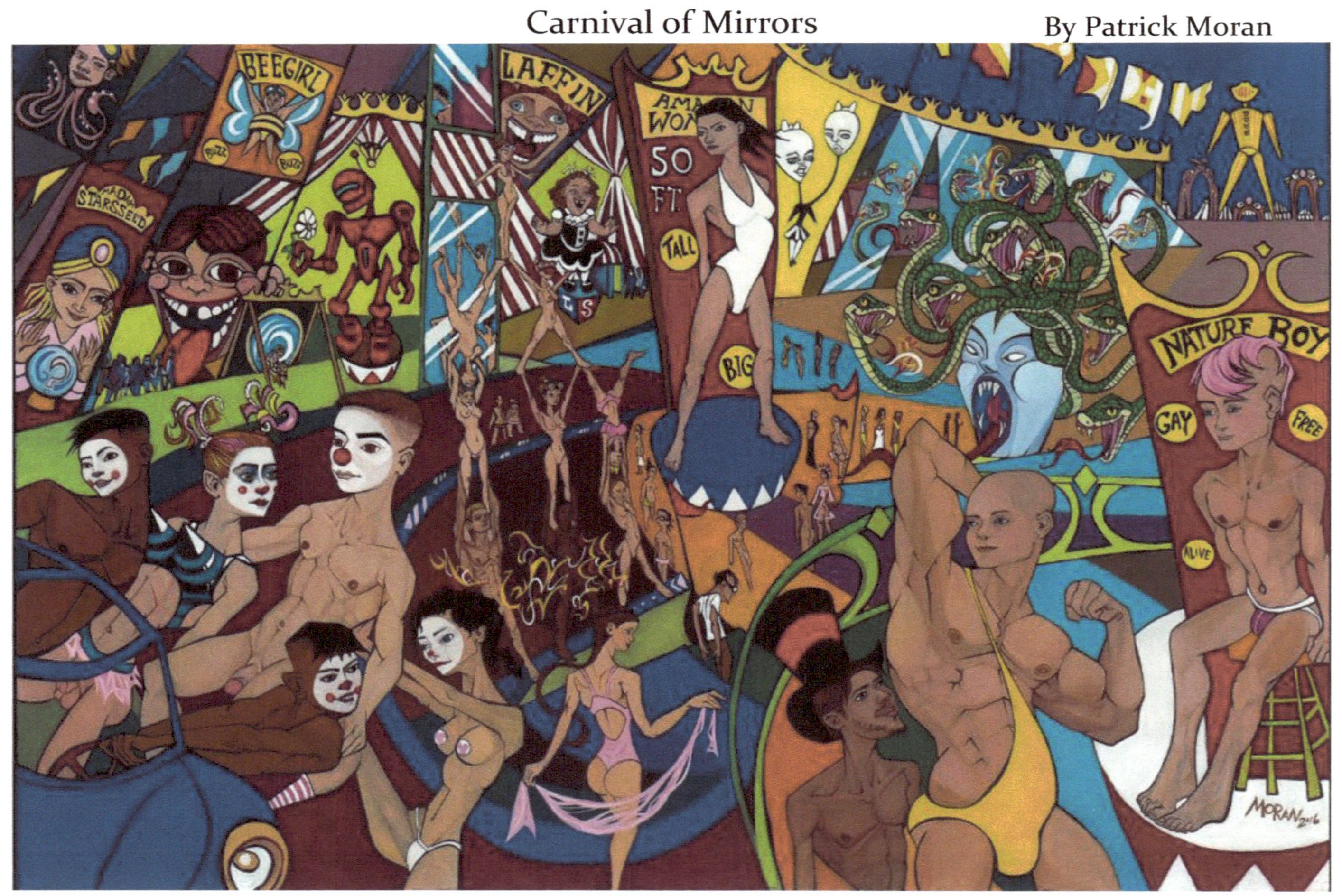

Once Upon a Festival

By Patrick Moran

Belden

By Patrick Moran

Note from the Author:

MORAN is an award winning artist working in California U.S.A. Paintings are created with the participation of models at during music and art festivals across the Western United States. Patrick J. Moran http://www.morangallery.com

Once Upon A Festival features "Bubbles" who was a fragile invincible eclectic unlimited free spirit artist. "Shut Up and Dance"

                                    CW: None

Lonely in California
By Justin Andrew Beale

Note from the Author:

Justin Andrew Beale is a Madison, Wisconsin based painter and ceramicist. His work draws influence from the Bay Area Funk movement, exploring queer theory, identity, color, texture, and form.

Justin Andrew Beale (@justinandrewbeale)

www.justinandrewbeale.com

Bible School

By David Russo

Sinful weenie, dirty muff,
catch some faggots by the scruff.
If they scream they've had enough,
remember Jesus likes it rough.

When they prance upon their hooves,
don't be swayed by artful moves.
If they say they need to dance,
remind them Hell will give the chance.

The devil waits for demons born
of lust, and hate and willful scorn
for Heaven's light and righteous roar,
to fire doomed forever more.

My First Crush

By David Russo

Surrounded by the Adirondacks,
Scout camp huddled under
blankets of pine needles,
wild blueberries, wintergreen.
King and Kennedy were gone,
we were one year from the moon.
Born To Be Wild blared from radios,
selling liberation to men and boys.
I was buying, that Summer of 1968,
when a 16-year-old red haired boy,

with fuzzy legs and pouty lips,
rattled my already-confused existence.

Jerry coached fitness class.
For two weeks he drove me hard,
shocked my muscles into surrender.
I endured because his proximity excited
within me the queerest throbs and tingles,
and visualized our last session,
that seemingly far-off day
when he would take my measurements.
The day arrived.
Soaking storms brought us to his cabin.
The tape measure caressed my calves,
crawled up my thighs, set me trembling.
Every part of me was congested.
I wanted to kiss him, hard and forever.
To a tenderfoot boy,
deceived by unfocused hopes,
a touch is an embrace,
until it vanishes like a ghost into timber and dust.

Cold Rain 1989
By David Russo

Clubs, cafes, street corners,
places to gather where we laughed, lied,
diluted our loneliness with that of others.
These streets were our Universe,
where suns consumed themselves,
stars streaked across the sky,

light fading before we even noticed.
The radiant, pulsating joy
infected us with impossible thoughts
of golden days, uncurbed nights.

Today I sit at that same corner
alone with my dreams of those times.
A dense fog slithers in,
turns cold drizzle,
dampens yesterday's memories,
baptizes me in truth.
Shuffling through the drops,
men are enshrouded in gray.
Wet shirts cling to bodies
that haunt their clothes.

If they have a home,
does anyone wait there?
Or are they unmissed,
dead to families even before
the virus takes them?

I have had enough of this parade.
I will not open my umbrella.
Still unscathed,
I can rush home.
I step into darkness,
shed saturated clothes,
surrender to my mattress and its empty valley.

Japanese Garden
By David Russo

Time rushes over the edge,
carrying with it the years
and memories of lives shared.

The current sweeps them over,
they plunge down to scatter the koi,
shatter the blue glassy calm
with the sound of shadows on water.

Buddha dreams in the grotto,
oblivious to the lovers more
connected to each other
than he is to the Universe.

Note from the Author:

David Russo, a retired attorney, enjoying a second career in the creative world. A committed social activist, he is a member of SAG-AFTRA and has appeared in commercials, television, theater, film and has written and produced. The poem Neighborhood, a selection from his current full-length book, The Poetic Heart, has been presented to the Mayor and

City Council of Long Beach, CA. His chapbook, Tokin' Of My Esteem: Hybrid Theory, will be released in August, 2017. His next full-length book, Leap Before You Look, is expected in late 2018. His poetry deeply confessional and evocative. Themes of difference, the nature of love, polyamory, sex and society, run throughout his work, which has been praised as multi-layered yet accessible to the reader. His frequent collaborations with visual artists are well known in California.

With his husband and two daughters, he moved from upstate New York and has lived in Long Beach, California for over twenty-two years. He is a grandfather of four.

A Love Letter
By Mindy Williams

A love-letter to
The universe.
I remember writing
Years ago, I kissed
You first –
And I remember forehead battles
Wrinkles like the sun.
Worry-warts. Things were simpler
Then.
A laugh like an orgasm at simple battle.

Note from the Author:

I forget how I would describe myself. I've lived in Hillcrest, the gayborhood, on and off for many years. I like Camille Paglia. And Route 66!

 CW: None

Stronger Together
By Kayleigh Russell

Stand together
Fall as one
When darkness wakes
Our time has come
Stand and fight
Or surrender now
But one thing's for sure
We won't back down

These are my rights
You cannot take those away
I will stand and fight
Until my very last day
So don't think you've won
We've only just begun
And we've got a larger army
Than you could ever fathom

We lurk in the shadows
In a world unseen
Discarded by you
Like the cause of disease
But we're stronger together
You'll never understand
What it's like to stand as one
Joined hand in hand
Because you've never been loyal
To anyone but yourself
So when you crash and burn
We will see you in hell

Note from the Author:

I am 24 years old, from Oxfordshire, England. I am currently studying at University and will hopefully move on to a degree in creative writing and film/tv studies, which I intend to use to create positive representation for LGBT+.

BECOME A PART OF OUR QUEER COMMUNITY

Our community of creators always needs new voices to add to the zine. Want to become a part of LOUD & QUEER?

Submit your writing, art, or other creations to:

loudandqueerzine@gmail.com

Please include 1) your name, 2) the name of your piece(s), and 3) 1-2 sentences to share with our readers.

We will consider your work for our next issue!

Share our call for submissions with LGBTQIA+ creators everywhere so we can give them a voice too!

THANK YOU to all the artists, writers, and creators who submitted their work and featured their pieces in LOUD & QUEER. The zine wouldn't be possible without you!

SUPPORT
LOUD & QUEER
NOW & FOREVER

LOUD & QUEER is committed to giving a voice to the queer community and projecting those perspectives into the wider community. We want everyone to hear queer voices of now, and that is why our zine is given out freely to all that want to read it.

We rely on patrons and donations to keep the zine going. Did you love this issue? Want new issues of LOUD & QUEER in the future? Want to receive exclusive perks and rewards while supporting LGBTQIA+ creators?

Become a patron of LOUD & QUEER
PATREON.COM/LOUDANDQUEERZINE

Marisa Wohlschlaeger